AF593499

Santa's Priority

By Tom Peterson

Illustrated by Michael LaVoy

Illustrations and graphic design by Michael LaVoy

ISBN: 978-1-5051-1597-0

Published in the United States by
TAN Books
P. O. Box 410487
Charlotte, NC 28241
www.TANBooks.com
Printed and bound in the United States of America

This book is dedicated to our wonderful grandchildren: RJ, Hannah, Savannah, Dominic, Lily, and any future grandbabies!

The angel said to them, “Do not be afraid; for behold, I proclaim to you good news of great joy that will be for all the people. For today in the city of David a savior has been born for you who is Messiah and Lord. And this will be a sign for you: you will find an infant wrapped in swaddling clothes and lying in a manger. And suddenly there was a multitude of the heavenly host with the angel, praising God and saying: Glory to God in the highest and on earth peace to those on whom his favor rests.   Luke 2:10-14

-T.P.

Thank you Maria, Weston, Vance, and Joseph for all your help!

-M.L.

Shining through darkness
Weston's Place
Van's
Abbi

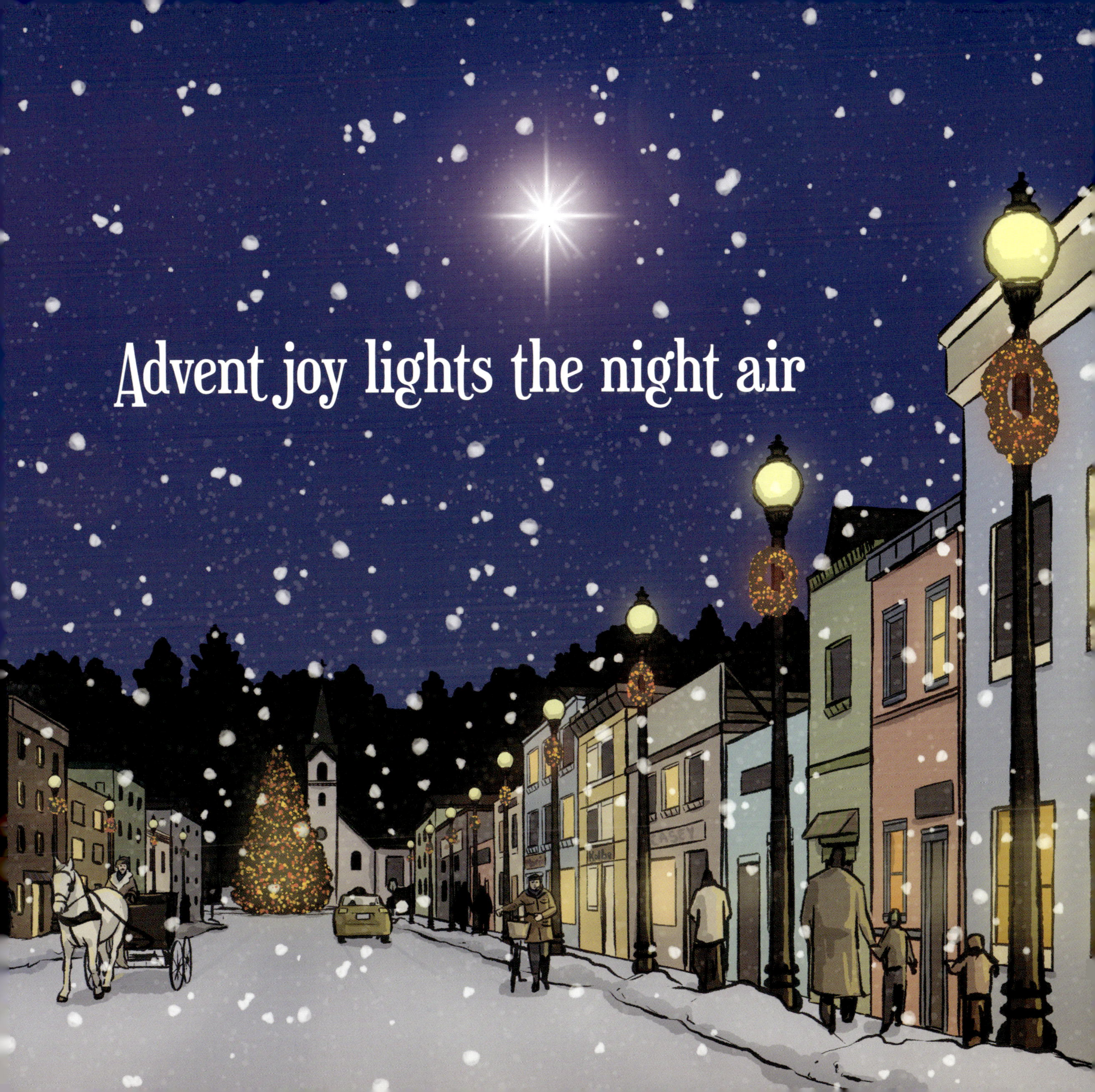
Advent joy lights the night air

for kindly St. Nicholas
was making his way there.

But wait for a moment,

there's a pause in his plan.

We're reminded Santa's priority

should be that
of every woman
and man.

For peace to flourish and love to abound,

Bakery

Our souls must come home,

the King of Kings must be found.

For centuries, Wise Men
sought the Savior first,

knowing only Jesus can quench
our heart's greatest thirst

So come home to Mass

and celebrate the holy Christian season.

For Love is born tonight,

our hope for Heaven, the reason.